SandCastle 3

Vowel Blends

Mary Elizabeth Salzmann

Published by SandCastle™, an imprint of ABDO Publishing Company, 4940 Viking Drive, Edina, Minnesota 55435.

Printed in the United States.

Cover and interior photo credits: Comstock, Digital Stock, Eyewire Images, Digital Vision, PhotoDisc, Photosphere, Stockbyte

Library of Congress Cataloging-in-Publication Data

Salzmann, Mary Elizabeth, 1968-
    Oo / Mary Elizabeth Salzmann.
      p. cm. -- (Vowel blends)
    ISBN 1-57765-457-9
    1. Readers (Primary) [1. English language--Phonetics.] I. Title.

PE1119 .S23424 2001
428.1--dc21

                                                                00-056569

The SandCastle concept, content, and reading method have been reviewed and approved by a national advisory board including literacy specialists, librarians, elementary school teachers, early childhood education professionals, and parents.

Let Us Know

After reading the book, SandCastle would like you to tell us your stories about reading. What is your favorite page? Was there something hard that you needed help with? Share the ups and downs of learning to read. We want to hear from you! To get posted on the ABDO Publishing Company Web site, send us email at:

sandcastle@abdopub.com

About SandCastle™

Nonfiction books for the beginning reader

- Basic concepts of phonics are incorporated with integrated language methods of reading instruction. Most words are short, and phrases, letter sounds, and word sounds are repeated.

- Readability is determined by the number of words in each sentence, the number of characters in each word, and word lists based on curriculum frameworks.

- Full-color photography reinforces word meanings and concepts.

- "Words I Can Read" list at the end of each book teaches basic elements of grammar, helps the reader recognize the words in the text, and builds vocabulary.

- Reading levels are indicated by the number of flags on the castle.

Look for more SandCastle books in these three reading levels:

Level 1 (one flag)	**Level 2** (two flags)	**Level 3** (three flags)
Grades Pre-K to K 5 or fewer words per page	**Grades K to 1** 5 to 10 words per page	**Grades 1 to 2** 10 to 15 words per page

Boone has fun staying cool in his pool.

It is a hot day.

Boothe likes to shoot marbles.

They are round and smooth.

oo

Tootie skis through
a hoop.

It is covered with many
colorful balloons.

Dooley and his brother like to go hiking.

They hike in the woods.

Oona has a pooch named Boomer.

Sometimes she gives him a smooch.

Rooney likes to shoot hoops with his grandpa.

They play after school.

Swoozie and Booker are in the school library.

They look for good books.

17

Brooke spins two hula hoops on the beach in the afternoon.

What kind of animal are Brooklyn and Cooper feeding?

(rooster)

Words I Can Read

Nouns

A noun is a person, place, or thing

afternoon (af-tur-NOON) p. 19
animal (AN-uh-muhl) p. 21
balloons (buh-LOONZ) p. 9
beach (BEECH) p. 19
books (BUKSS) p. 17
brother (BRUHTH-ur) p. 11

day (DAY) p. 5
fun (FUHN) p. 5
grandpa (GRAND-pa) p. 15
hoop (HOOP) p. 9
hoops (HOOPSS) p. 15
hula hoops (HOO-luh hoopss) p. 19
kind (KINDE) p. 21

library (LYE-brer-ee) p. 17
marbles (MAR-buhlz) p. 7
pooch (POOCH) p. 13
pool (POOL) p. 5
rooster (ROO-stur) p. 21
school (SKOOL) p. 15
smooch (SMOOCH) p. 13
woods (WUDZ) p. 11

Proper Nouns

A proper noun is the name of a person, place, or thing

Booker (BUK-ur) p. 17
Boomer (BOO-mur) p. 13
Boone (BOON) p. 5
Boothe (BOOTH) p. 7

Brooke (BRUK) p. 19
Brooklyn (BRUK-lin) p. 21
Cooper (KOO-pur) p. 21
Dooley (DOO-lee) p. 11

Oona (OO-nuh) p. 13
Rooney (ROO-nee) p. 15
Swoozie (SWOO-zee) p. 17
Tootie (TOO-tee) p. 9

Pronouns

A pronoun is a word that replaces a noun

him (HIM) p. 13
it (IT) pp. 5, 9

she (SHEE) p. 13
they (THAY) pp. 7, 11, 15, 17

what (WUHT) p. 21

22

Verbs

A verb is an action or being word

are (AR) pp. 7, 17, 21
covered (KUHV-urd) p. 9
feeding (FEED-ing) p. 21
gives (GIVZ) p. 13
go (GOH) p. 11
has (HAZ) pp. 5, 13

hike (HIKE) p. 11
hiking (HIKE-ing) p. 11
is (IZ) pp. 5, 9
like (LIKE) p. 11
likes (LIKESS) pp. 7, 15
look (LUK) p. 17

named (NAYMD) p. 13
play (PLAY) p. 15
shoot (SHOOT)
    pp. 7, 15
skis (SKEEZ) p. 9
spins (SPINZ) p. 19
staying (STAY-ing) p. 5

Adjectives

An adjective describes something

colorful (KUHL-ur-ful) p. 9
cool (KOOL) p. 5
good (GUD) p. 17
his (HIZ) pp. 5, 11, 15

hot (HOT) p. 5
many (MEN-ee) p. 9
round (ROUND) p. 7
school (SKOOL) p. 17

smooth (SMOOTH) p. 7
two (TOO) p. 19

Adverbs

An adverb tells how, when, or where something happens

sometimes
    (SUHM-timez) p. 13

23

Glossary

hula hoops – Plastic hoops that are twirled around the body.

marbles – Small glass balls used in a children's game.

pooch – Another word for dog.

rooster – A fully-grown male chicken.

smooch – Another word for kiss.

More oo Words

baboon	goose	roof
boom	hoot	room
boot	kangaroo	soon
choose	moon	spoon
door	moose	tool
floor	poor	tooth
food	racoon	zoo

24